A Worship Journal
for Biblical Counseling

A Worship Journal
for Biblical Counseling

Rick Witmer

A Worship Journal for Biblical Counseling

ISBN: 979-8-218-28966-9

To my counselees.

Serving you in your moments of greatest vulnerability
is one of the most profound privileges of my life.

"Blessed be the God and Father of our Lord Jesus Christ,
the Father of mercies and God of all comfort,
who comforts us in all our tribulation,
that we may be able to comfort those who are in any trouble,
with the comfort with which we ourselves are comforted by God."
2 Corinthians 1:3-4

Table of Contents

Using *A Worship Journal*
for Biblical Counseling

I suppose I should tell you from the outset that you don't need to be in biblical counseling to use this journal, though I created the journal with counselees in mind. If you look through the journal pages, you'll quickly see that this book is simply a guided walk through your daily time in the Bible and prayer. If you would like some structure for daily time with God, then this journal is for you!

Biblical Counseling

I've been a counselor for almost 15 years (at the time I'm writing this), and for the past 13 of those years I've been committed to biblical counseling. I was trained in clinical counseling and marriage and family therapy, and biblical counseling as an approach to helping people was never even mentioned at my Christian graduate school. It wasn't until the Lord called me to the pastorate that I was exposed to the foundational work of men such as Jay Adams, David Powlison, Paul Tripp, Ed Welch, and others. It didn't take long for me to realize that the biblical counseling movement was the home I was searching for and had never found in the world of psychotherapy. I've never looked back!

Countless scores of counseling theories and philosophies abound, but only one begins with the triune God, His Bible, and the Gospel as the foundation and substance of how to solve problems—*biblical counseling*. A truly Christian approach to helping people seeks to frame all of life's problems and solutions in the grand story of what God has done to save sinners like us through His Son, Jesus Christ. Biblical counseling rests on the sufficiency of the Bible for making sense of our struggles and how we can grow in godliness through them (including the "big ones" like bipolar disorder, depression, OCD, and severe anxiety[1]).

Biblical counselors and their counselees look to the Bible and seek God for the Holy Spirit's vital ministry in working through the challenges and opportunities of life. The goal of all biblical counseling is the glory of God and the good of the counselee, and is dependent on the Holy Spirit. It honors the complex unity of body and soul, recognizing that sometimes the struggles we face include a medical element (which is why biblical counselors are quick to refer counselees to their doctors for evaluation and treatment of physiological issues). Yet however profound the struggle and whatever the interplay between body and soul, counseling should always be centered on the person and work of Jesus Christ. This is true for several reasons, and sets the foundation for understanding why *A Worship Journal for Biblical Counseling* is a helpful tool, regardless of the issue on the table.

First, **all of life is about Jesus!** Whatever problems we face, Jesus has everything to do with how we navigate them. The Apostle Paul shows us this in majestic and almost poetic language:

> He is the image of the invisible God, the firstborn over all creation. For by Him all things were created that are in heaven and that are on earth, visible and invisible, whether thrones or dominions or principalities or powers. *All things were created through Him and for Him.* And He is before all things, and *in Him all things consist.* (Colossians 1:15-17, emphasis mine)

The conclusion that Christ is the center of everything is inescapable. Applied to counseling in particular, it isn't too much to say that every counselee (including their problems) is created through Jesus and exists

---

[1] A helpful book that demonstrates the real-world sufficiency of Scripture for issues that are traditionally believed to be the domain of psychologists and professional counselors is Stuart Scott and Heath Lambert's edited volume, *Counseling the Hard Cases: True Stories Illustrating the Sufficiency of God's Resources in Scripture* (Nashville, TN: B&H Academic, 2015).

for Jesus and holds together in Jesus—therefore, Jesus has everything to do with counseling.

Second, **every counselee will stand before the Judgment Seat of Christ.** Paul was no stranger to affliction. In fact, I think the psychiatric community might have a field day analyzing Paul's life for themes of PTSD, depression, anxiety, and self-destructive tendencies! We get some incredibly personal autobiographical information from Paul in 2 Corinthians, watching him suffer in profound ways as he seeks to make much of Jesus. In writing to the Church in Corinth about suffering, he referred to our bodies as "tents," saying:

> For in this we groan, earnestly desiring to be clothed with our habitation which is from heaven, if indeed, having been clothed, we shall not be found naked. For we who are in this tent groan, being burdened, not because we want to be unclothed, but further clothed, that mortality may be swallowed up by life. Now He who has prepared us for this very thing is God, who also has given us the Spirit as a guarantee. So we are always confident, knowing that while we are at home in the body we are absent from the Lord. For we walk by faith, not by sight. We are confident, yes, well pleased rather to be absent from the body and to be present with the Lord. *Therefore we make it our aim, whether present or absent, to be well pleasing to Him. For we must all appear before the judgment seat of Christ, that each one may receive the things done in the body, according to what he has done, whether good or bad.* (2 Corinthians 5:2-10, emphasis mine)

Every single counselee is accountable to God as one of His image-bearers, and Lord-willing, as one of His redeemed children. Whatever suffering is being addressed in counseling, whatever habits or struggles or broken relationships, we know that each counselee will stand before God one day and give an account of his or her life. While addressing the whole person—body and soul—we can know with biblical certainty that the ultimate aim of counseling (according to Paul) must be to help every counselee respond to their life circumstances and struggles in a way that is pleasing to God. In this, God gets the greatest glory and the counselee will work toward their greatest good.

Finally (though there are several other good reasons for Christ being the center of counseling), **every counseling struggle is part of the great story arc of Redemptive History.** We all live in a context. No one exists in isolation. That means that we must seek to understand our lives in their proper setting. From God's perspective—and I would *always* suggest taking God's perspective if given the chance—everything falls somewhere along the great storyline of the Bible, commonly broken down into four "acts":

Creation

God the Father, Son, and Holy Spirit create all things for His glory, perfect and without blemish. At the apex of His creation is Adam and Eve, who are created to glorify, love, obey, and enjoy God as they exercise authority as His vice-regents to cultivate His very good world. (This is the story told by Genesis 1-2.)

Fall

Tempted by the serpent, Adam and Eve rebel against God. In consequence of violating God's holy law, they (together with all their descendants, save only Jesus Christ) experience spiritual and physical death. (This is the story told by Genesis 3 and that we see at play throughout the rest of Scripture.)

Redemption

In His eternal wisdom and gracious love, God the Father chose to redeem undeserving sinners through His Son, Jesus Christ. The eternal Son of God entered human history in the Incarnation, taking to Himself a true human nature (except for sin) and living the perfect life under God's law that no one could, dying the death His people deserve, and rising from the dead after fully satisfying God's just wrath for their sins. He ascended to heaven and is enthroned at the right hand of the Father, making His enemies a footstool for His feet and interceding for

His saints until He comes to judge all humanity and dwell with His people in the New Heavens and New Earth. The Holy Spirit is faithfully drawing to God all those for whom Christ died, and He accomplishes God's will in the world. (This redemption is promised all throughout the Old Testament, played out in the Gospels, and expounded in the Epistles.)

Restoration

In God's perfect time and way, Christ will return and make all things new. Sin, Satan, Christ-rejecters, and death will be cast into the lake of fire forever, and the kingdom will be delivered to God the Father as the saints enjoy the New Heavens and New Earth with God forever and ever! (This is promised all through the Old and New Testaments, and seen especially in places like 1 Corinthians 15 and Revelation 21-22.)

That is the arc of the whole Bible, and every one of us are found in that story. Whatever sin or suffering each of us deals with, it all fits somewhere in that story. If you're paying attention, you will have noticed that the story is heading in a very particular direction—the glory of the God who is making all things new (Revelation 21:5). And if that's the big picture of where our lives are headed, counseling that is distinctly Christian can do no better than to honor and address the depths of pain, sorrow, and sin in light of what is ultimate. This is where the centrality of worship comes in....

A Worship Journal for Biblical Counseling

In the years I've practiced counseling, I've found one common thread that is true for numerous counselees, if not most: *Meaningful time in worship is minimal or almost altogether lacking.* I know that this isn't the case only for my counselees, either; this is a universal problem seen by all biblical counselors. It's certainly not the case with every counselee, but it is with many.

When I talk about meaningful time in worship, I'm primarily referring to what I call "secret worship" (or individual/private worship). The substance of secret worship is our reading of and meditation on God's Word, and responding to what He says in His Word through prayer. This is almost certainly the most daunting part of the Christian life for many believers, which is why it is so often neglected. Throw in life problems of any significance, and whatever time we give to our personal relationship with the Lord easily falls by the wayside.

If Christ must be the center of counseling, then cultivating our relationship with Him through Word and prayer must be the "bread and butter" of whatever else happens in counseling. Wherever knowing Christ is not at the heart of the change process, the change will either be short-lived or it will be built on a foundation of sand. The wise man builds his house on the rock, and that rock is Christ (Matthew 7:24-25).

One of the most helpful ways to cultivate a habit of communion with Christ is through intention and planning. I often tell my counselees that if I could have one thing engraved on my headstone when I die by which I would be remembered, it would be this: FAITHFULNESS DOESN'T HAPPEN ACCIDENTALLY. Time after time I've witnessed good intentions fall flat because there was no plan or vision for what faithfulness looks like. This journal aims to fill the gap of "plan-lessness."

I also intend the journal to be a ready-to-go resource for biblical counselors to hand to their counselees as an ongoing homework assignment throughout the first month of the counseling process. It is divided into four weeks of five days. Each day has space to record what parts of Scripture were read, guide a counselee through engaging meditatively with the Scripture, and then bridge the gap from meditation into prayer. For the weeks it is used, it hits at the elements of secret worship to help whoever is using it get into a steady habit of communion with Christ. There is also a spot at the end of each day for a counselee to write out a Scripture passage that their counselor has assigned them to memorize. Lastly, because faithful involvement in corporate worship is an essential part of the Christian life (as well as the counseling process), there is a page for sermon notes at the beginning of each week's journal.

Meditating With Luther

As someone who falls squarely in the Reformed tradition, I am deeply indebted to and grateful for Martin Luther, the theologian-professor-monk whom God used to spark the Protestant Reformation in 1517. For all the flaws and peccadillos in Luther's life (of which there were many), he was a Christ-centered man of prayer second to none.

I've benefited greatly from a short little book he wrote for his barber, in which he responds to his barber's request to teach him to pray. In that booklet, *A Simple Way to Pray*[2], Luther teaches how to walk the path from Bible to meditation to prayer. By meditation, Luther does not mean "emptying the mind and seeing where the Spirit leads" or anything like that. Rather, the Scriptures guide the meditation, as we mull over what God has revealed in the Bible about Himself, our sin, His gracious blessings, and Christ. This journal is informed by Luther's way to pray.

Luther understood that whatever else a person may be, he is never more than his prayer life. Speaking of the importance of prayer, Luther once famously remarked, "I have so much to do that I shall spend the first three hours in prayer!" He also knew that prayer was a challenge. In *A Simple Way to Pray* he wrote:

> First, sometimes I feel I am becoming cold and apathetic about prayer. This is usually because of all the things that are distracting me and filling my mind. I know this is a result of the flesh and the devil always waging war against me, trying to prevent me from praying. When this happens I like to take my little book of the Psalms and sneak away into a little room, or, if it is the right time or day, I like to go to church with other people....
>
> This is why it is such a good idea to start your day, first thing, early in the morning, by praying, and then make it the last thing you do at the end of the day. This way you can prevent lying to yourself by

---

[2] Martin Luther, *A Simple Way to Pray*, transl. by Matthew C. Harrison (St. Louis, MO: Concordia Publishing, 2012).

saying, "Oh, I can wait a little while. I'll pray in an hour or so, but first I need to do this or that." It is this kind of thinking that will have you believe something is actually better, or more important, than prayer, particularly if some emergency demands your attention....

We have to be absolutely certain that we do not allow ourselves to be distracted from genuine prayer.

It's good to know that such a godly man as Martin Luther struggled in prayer, and that he was also—by God's grace—successful in prayer. It means that we too can have a thriving prayer life with God's help! Something similar is said about the prophet Elijah: "The effective, fervent prayer of a righteous man avails much. Elijah was a man with a nature like ours, and he prayed earnestly that it would not rain; and it did not rain on the land for three years and six months." (James 5:16b-17) The famous saints of days past had the same access to God's presence and the same Holy Spirit that you and I have, and that is a great encouragement to prayer.

As you have morning worship, I'd like to briefly share how Martin Luther prayed, so that you may connect your Bible study with your prayer life. He used the following method for any given passage of the Bible:

(1) Begin by spending a moment remembering who God is and praising Him for some of His perfections (attributes— qualities like His eternal nature, His divine power, His saving love, His triunity, etc.).

(2) Then ask Him to meet you in His Word, opening your eyes to the wonders of the Bible (Psalm 119:18).

(3) Now, go to the Word and spend some time working on whatever passage(s) are next in your reading plan.

God speaks to us in His Word. Now, how do you respond to Him? *In prayer.* Luther gave a simple way to move from God's Word into

16

meaningful prayer. In the introduction to his translation of *A Simple Way to Pray*, Matthew Harrison boils down Luther's method to what he calls, "I.T.C.P."[3] Here's how it works—using the Bible text you've just read, pick a portion to meditate on in the following way:

Instruction

Talk with God about what the passage teaches you about Him. Perhaps it reveals something about you and your need for Him? Do you see Jesus there in some way? God's attributes—His justice, love, wrath, mercy, covenant faithfulness, etc.? Spend a moment talking with God in prayer about what He is teaching you with the words that He wrote for you in this portion of the Bible.

Thanksgiving

Thank God personally for what He has said, promised, and communicated to you. Everywhere we look in Scripture, God is constantly communicating His character, goodness, and blessings to us. If we're not thanking Him for these things, then we're not listening.

Confession

God being Who He is—the Holy Majesty of Heaven—sheds some serious light on who we are: *great sinners in need of a great Savior*. Look through your passage and consider what commands God has given there, and then examine your own life. Have you matched up with what He's said? Spend time confessing your sins to God, asking Him to give you a soft heart that is grieved by your sin, and place your whole trust in Jesus Christ alone. You cannot save yourself or earn your way to God's presence. Confession is your owning up to that and trusting that Christ earned the way for you in His perfect life, death, and resurrection. Your confession of sin should be as specific as you

---

[3] Ibid., 3.

can make it, which is why thinking about the specific words of God in your chapter is helpful.

Prayer

Even though you've been praying this whole time as you meditate on God's Word, this time in prayer is for things and people that come to mind as you are working through Scripture. For example, at the end of Ephesians 1 there is a rich prayer that Paul prays for the Christians he's writing to, and maybe you could think about praying those things for Christians you know—your friends, parents, pastors, etc. Pray for what's on your heart, needs that have been on your mind, and finish your set aside time of prayer acknowledging God's greatness by bringing anything and everything before Him until your time is up.

The journal for each day will guide you through this process of meditating on Scripture and responding in prayer. There will be places for you to record a prayer, or to take notes on things you pray about. If writing is a struggle for you, then don't feel pressured to write long or polished prayers. The goal isn't filling out the journal, but rather cultivating a growing relationship with God through Christ. If you merely write some notes in the sections to keep track of your thoughts on Scripture and the content of your prayers, that's a win, too! If you are using this journal in the context of biblical counseling, I would encourage you to do at least that, because your counselor will likely want to see how you are engaging God through His Word.

Where Are You With Christ?

This journal is all about spending time with the Lord through His Word and prayer. This presupposes something so essential that without it, the task ahead is impossible: *that you truly know Christ*. The Bible was inspired by the Holy Spirit, and while anyone may read it, only those who have spiritual life through Christ will truly understand and benefit from it: "But the natural man does not receive the things of the Spirit of God, for they are foolishness to him; nor can he know them, because they are spiritually discerned" (1 Corinthians 2:14).

Earlier in these pages I explained to you the great story told by the Bible, which includes the Gospel of Jesus Christ. Paul summarizes this Gospel in 1 Corinthians 15 when he writes:

> Moreover, brethren, I declare to you the gospel which I preached to you, which also you received and in which you stand, by which also you are saved, if you hold fast that word which I preached to you—unless you believed in vain. For I delivered to you first of all that which I also received: that Christ died for our sins according to the Scriptures, and that He was buried, and that He rose again the third day according to the Scriptures, and that He was seen by Cephas, then by the twelve. (vv 1-5)

Dear reader, I don't know who you are, what your life is like, or where you are in relation to this Gospel that Paul declared. I trust that if you are in biblical counseling, your counselor is attentive to these things. However, I know that not all who pick up this little journal will be in an ongoing relationship with a biblical counselor. Whoever you are and whatever your situation, I would simply ask, *Where are you with Christ?*

Do you know and believe that you are a great sinner who is condemned before the Holy One apart from faith in Christ alone? Do you trust in the perfect and finished work that Jesus has done on the cross for you? Is your faith in Christ a repentant faith that has turned from the sin you once loved to now follow Him by the Spirit's help? Have you responded to the call of Christ, who came preaching, "The time is fulfilled, and the kingdom of God is at hand. Repent, and believe in the gospel" (Mark 1:15)?

If you trust in Christ by repentant faith, the Scriptures declare that you have been born again (John 3:3-8), your sins are forgiven (1 John 1:9), you have been washed by the Holy Spirit (1 Corinthians 6:11), and you are a new creation (2 Corinthians 5:17)! You have the mind of Christ (1 Corinthians 2:14), and as you prayerfully meditate on God's Word in the days ahead, you can look forward to the work Your heavenly Father will do in you through Christ and by His Spirit. Your faith is a faith that will bear fruit (James 2:14-26), and you are on the path to greater fruitfulness as you draw near to God.

If, however, you do not trust in Christ by repentant faith, then I plead with you to turn from your sins and embrace the great Savior who alone can save you! "Seek the LORD while He may be found, call upon Him while He is near. Let the wicked forsake his way, and the unrighteous man his thoughts; let him return to the LORD, and He will have mercy on him, and to our God, for He will abundantly pardon" (Isaiah 55:6-7). The one true God is a gracious God, and He promises to receive you if you come to Him through faith in Christ. "Jesus said to him, 'I am the way, the truth, and the life. No one comes to the Father except through Me" (John 14:6).

I wonder if perhaps some reader or other has associated with Christ but never truly followed him—identifying as a Christian without actually *being* a Christian through obedient faith. Jesus warns at the end of the Sermon on the Mount, "Not everyone who says to Me, 'Lord, Lord,' shall enter the kingdom of heaven, but he who does the will of My Father in heaven" (Matthew 7:21). If that's you, I likewise plead with you to turn to the Lord and seek Him while He may be found! Jesus warns us of the possibility of false faith not to condemn us, but because He wants us to turn to Him from false faith and have life. As you read, meditate on, and pray Scripture in the days ahead, do so with a spirit of dependence on Christ and a determination with His help to obey what He says. You will be truly blessed as you do.

May we each know where we are with Christ as we press on.

Thanks and Blessing

I pray this journal would be a fruitful tool for God's glory in your life and for your joy. Thank you for taking the time to read this short introductory chapter, and may you grow in the grace and knowledge of the Lord Jesus Christ and see His sufficient grace abound in your life (2 Peter 3:18; 2 Corinthians 12:9)!

Worship Journal

A Sample Journal Entry

To show how this method for prayer works from any given passage of Scripture, I took the opportunity on the morning that I wrote this to worship from the first chapter I came to in my daily Old Testament reading. I hope it is useful to get a sense of how this can work as a helpful aid in approaching God through His Word.

Always remember to spend a moment praising God for who He is and asking for His Spirit's aid in understanding what you're reading in His Word.

It would be helpful if you paused for a moment to read 2 Kings 1 so you can see what I'm seeing.

NOTE: Some of the following sections are more detailed than typical because I want you to see both the flow of the story and the flow of my thoughts as I meditate. You will usually be briefer in some of the sections (like Main Ideas or Applications).

Bible Passage: 2 Kings 1

Main ideas I see in this passage:

King Ahaziah in Israel injures himself and is bed-bound, yet instead of seeking the Lord he idolatrously seeks Baal (v 2). This leads to God sending Elijah to prophesy Ahaziah's death in consequence of his idolatry (vv 3-4). As Ahaziah sends three companies of soldiers, the Lord shows His might by consuming with fire the companies who represented Ahaziah's kingly authority (vv 5-12). Only when the third captain humbles himself does the Lord spare him and send Elijah to Ahaziah to declare his impending death again, which comes to pass (vv 13-18). I understand the Angel of the Lord (vv 3, 15) to be the Son of God manifest before His incarnation. The main ideas I see from this chapter are: **(1)** Ahaziah dies not primarily because of his injury, but as divine judgment for his idolatry. **(2)** Yahweh is mightier than any king or military—He is King of kings. **(3)** The Lord is involved in the details of our lives, even using normal life circumstances (like injuries) to accomplish His will. **(4)** Ahaziah should have humbled himself before the Lord, as the third captain did.

Key Verse(s):

"But the angel of the LORD said to Elijah the Tishbite, 'Arise, go up to meet the messengers of the king of Samaria, and say to them, "Is it because there is no God in Israel that you are going to inquire of Baal-Zebub, the god of Ekron?" (2 Kings 1:3)

Being a doer of the Word: What applications are there for me?

(1) I must always seek the Lord and guard against the temptation to idolatrously trust in technology, modern medicine, investments, or other sources of comfort—unlike Baal, these things are fine in themselves, but it is easy to turn to them in my trials instead of turning to Christ. **(2)** It would be frightening to face down three companies of soldiers, but Elijah had confidence in the Lord's power to deliver him; I must fight anxiety and fear by trusting in the Lord. **(3)** "Humble yourselves in the sight of the Lord, and He will lift you up" (James 4:10).

What sins should I confess and repent of through Christ?

(1) I easily give lip service to trusting God while trying to make sure my circumstances, bank accounts, and plans hedge against discomfort or trouble—I often fail to truly trust God with my life. **(2)** It is natural for me to be proud rather than humble.

What should I ask God to help me believe, think, and/or do?

That I would truly believe that Christ is the powerful King at the Father's right hand who rules over this world and my life (Psalm 110:1-2); and that I would show this belief in an attitude of genuine trust, especially when things aren't going my way.

Prayer

Instruction:

Lord, You confronted Ahaziah's idolatry by sending Elijah to prophesy Ahaziah's death, and You consumed two companies of soldiers who did not show the fear of the Lord. You are the mighty King to be feared and honored! The only right response to You is humble worship. Lord Christ, You are at the center of the story, leading Elijah to do God's will. Truly, "our God is a consuming fire" (Hebrews 12:29).

Thanksgiving:

I praise and thank You for Your majesty shown in 2 Kings 1! There is no God like You, able to protect Your people and rule over the nations. Baal is no god, and every false god that man makes up is utterly futile. Your power is total, and You graciously call me to come before You in humble worship through Jesus Christ. Thank you for recording this story for my benefit, that I may enjoy true fellowship with You.

Confession:

Father, forgive my arrogant pride! How often do I reflexively trust in the things of earth to give me comfort, peace, and protection? I am much more like Ahaziah than I care to imagine, but I pray that You would forgive me and grant me the humility that pleases You. Help me to have the confidence in You that Elijah showed. Through Christ my Lord, who humbled Himself to death for my salvation and rose in victory. Amen.

Prayer:

(1) That world rulers would turn to Christ and be saved. **(2)** For people in my church facing anxiety-provoking circumstances. **(3)** That my wife and children and I would trust the Lord for our future, and that we would teach our children the greatness of God. **(4)** For the Persecuted Church. **(5)** For my counselees. **(6)** That the Church would be a bold witness. **(7)** Salvation for loved ones who don't know Christ.

Memory Verse(s):

"And when His disciples James and John saw this, they said, 'Lord, do You want us to command fire to come down from heaven and consume them, just as Elijah did?' But He turned and rebuked them, and said, 'You do not know what manner of spirit you are of. For the Son of Man did not come to destroy men's lives but to save them.'" (Luke 9:54-56a)

Week One

Sermon Notes

Date: _____

Preaching Passage: _____

Notes:

_____
_____
_____
_____
_____
_____
_____
_____
_____
_____
_____

Applications:

_____
_____
_____
_____
_____
_____

Day 1

Date: _____

Bible Passage: _____

Main ideas I see in this passage:

_____

_____

_____

_____

_____

_____

Key Verse(s):

_____

_____

_____

_____

_____

Being a doer of the Word: What applications are there for me?

_____

_____

_____

_____

_____

_____

_____

_____

_____

_____

What sins should I confess and repent of through Christ?

_____

_____

_____

_____

_____

_____

_____

What should I ask God to help me believe, think, and/or do?

_____

_____

_____

_____

_____

_____

_____

_____

Prayer

Instruction:

_____

_____

_____

_____

_____

_____

_____

_____

Thanksgiving:

_____

_____

_____

_____

_____

_____

_____

_____

Confession:

_____

_____

_____

_____

_____

_____

_____

_____

_____

Prayer:

_____

_____

_____

_____

_____

_____

_____

_____

Memory Verse(s):

_____

_____

_____

_____

_____

_____

Day 2

Date: _____

Bible Passage: _____

Main ideas I see in this passage:

_____

_____

_____

_____

_____

_____

Key Verse(s):

_____

_____

_____

_____

_____

_____

Being a doer of the Word: What applications are there for me?

_____

_____

_____

_____

_____

_____

_____

_____

_____

_____

What sins should I confess and repent of through Christ?

_____

_____

_____

_____

_____

_____

_____

What should I ask God to help me believe, think, and/or do?

_____

_____

_____

_____

_____

_____

_____

_____

Prayer

Instruction:

_____

_____

_____

_____

_____

_____

_____

_____

Thanksgiving:

_____

_____

_____

_____

_____

_____

_____

_____

Confession:

_____

_____

_____

_____

_____

_____

_____

_____

_____

Prayer:

_____

_____

_____

_____

_____

_____

_____

_____

_____

Memory Verse(s):

_____

_____

_____

_____

_____

_____

_____

Day 3

Date: _____

Bible Passage: _____

Main ideas I see in this passage:

_____

_____

_____

_____

_____

_____

Key Verse(s):

_____

_____

_____

_____

_____

Being a doer of the Word: What applications are there for me?

_____

_____

_____

_____

_____

_____

_____

_____

_____

_____

What sins should I confess and repent of through Christ?

_____

_____

_____

_____

_____

_____

_____

What should I ask God to help me believe, think, and/or do?

_____

_____

_____

_____

_____

_____

_____

_____

Prayer

Instruction:

_____
_____
_____
_____
_____
_____
_____
_____
_____
_____

Thanksgiving:

_____
_____
_____
_____
_____
_____
_____
_____
_____
_____

Confession:

_____
_____

_____
_____
_____
_____
_____
_____
_____

Prayer:

_____
_____
_____
_____
_____
_____
_____

Memory Verse(s):

_____
_____
_____
_____
_____
_____

Day 4

Date: _____

Bible Passage: _____

Main ideas I see in this passage:

_____

_____

_____

_____

_____

_____

Key Verse(s):

_____

_____

_____

_____

_____

Being a doer of the Word: What applications are there for me?

_____

_____

_____

_____

_____

_____

_____

_____

_____

_____

What sins should I confess and repent of through Christ?

_____

_____

_____

_____

_____

_____

_____

What should I ask God to help me believe, think, and/or do?

_____

_____

_____

_____

_____

_____

_____

_____

Prayer

Instruction:

_____

_____

_____

_____

_____

_____

_____

_____

Thanksgiving:

_____

_____

_____

_____

_____

_____

_____

_____

Confession:

_____

_____

_____

_____

_____

_____

_____

_____

_____

Prayer:

_____

_____

_____

_____

_____

_____

_____

_____

_____

Memory Verse(s):

_____

_____

_____

_____

_____

_____

_____

Day 5

Date: _____

Bible Passage: _____

Main ideas I see in this passage:

_____

_____

_____

_____

_____

_____

Key Verse(s):

_____

_____

_____

_____

_____

Being a doer of the Word: What applications are there for me?

_____

_____

_____

_____

_____

_____

_____

_____

_____

_____

What sins should I confess and repent of through Christ?

_____

_____

_____

_____

_____

_____

_____

What should I ask God to help me believe, think, and/or do?

_____

_____

_____

_____

_____

_____

_____

_____

Prayer

Instruction:

_____

_____

_____

_____

_____

_____

_____

_____

_____

Thanksgiving:

_____

_____

_____

_____

_____

_____

_____

_____

_____

Confession:

_____

_____

_____

_____

_____

_____

_____

_____

_____

Prayer:

_____

_____

_____

_____

_____

_____

_____

_____

Memory Verse(s):

_____

_____

_____

_____

_____

_____

Week Two

Sermon Notes

Date: _____

Preaching Passage: _____

Notes:

_____

_____

_____

_____

_____

_____

_____

_____

_____

_____

_____

_____

_____

Applications:

_____

_____

_____

_____

_____

_____

Day 6

Date: _____

Bible Passage: _____

Main ideas I see in this passage:

_____
_____
_____
_____
_____
_____

Key Verse(s):

_____
_____
_____
_____
_____
_____

Being a doer of the Word: What applications are there for me?

_____
_____
_____
_____

_____

_____

_____

_____

_____

_____

What sins should I confess and repent of through Christ?

_____

_____

_____

_____

_____

_____

What should I ask God to help me believe, think, and/or do?

_____

_____

_____

_____

_____

_____

_____

Prayer

Instruction:

_____

_____

_____

_____

_____

_____

_____

_____

Thanksgiving:

_____

_____

_____

_____

_____

_____

_____

Confession:

_____

_____

_____

_____

_____

_____

_____

_____

_____

Prayer:

_____

_____

_____

_____

_____

_____

_____

Memory Verse(s):

_____

_____

_____

_____

_____

_____

Day 7

Date: _____

Bible Passage: _____

Main ideas I see in this passage:

_____
_____
_____
_____
_____
_____

Key Verse(s):

_____
_____
_____
_____
_____

Being a doer of the Word: What applications are there for me?

_____
_____
_____
_____

_____

_____

_____

_____

_____

_____

What sins should I confess and repent of through Christ?

_____

_____

_____

_____

_____

_____

_____

What should I ask God to help me believe, think, and/or do?

_____

_____

_____

_____

_____

_____

_____

_____

Prayer

Instruction:

_____

_____

_____

_____

_____

_____

_____

_____

Thanksgiving:

_____

_____

_____

_____

_____

_____

_____

_____

Confession:

_____

_____

_____

_____

_____

_____

_____

_____

_____

Prayer:

_____

_____

_____

_____

_____

_____

_____

_____

Memory Verse(s):

_____

_____

_____

_____

_____

_____

Day 8

Date: _____

Bible Passage: _____

Main ideas I see in this passage:

_____

_____

_____

_____

_____

_____

Key Verse(s):

_____

_____

_____

_____

_____

_____

Being a doer of the Word: What applications are there for me?

_____

_____

_____

_____

_____
_____
_____
_____
_____
_____

What sins should I confess and repent of through Christ?

_____
_____
_____
_____
_____
_____
_____

What should I ask God to help me believe, think, and/or do?

_____
_____
_____
_____
_____
_____
_____
_____

Prayer

Instruction:

_____

_____

_____

_____

_____

_____

_____

_____

Thanksgiving:

_____

_____

_____

_____

_____

_____

_____

_____

Confession:

_____

_____

_____

_____

_____

_____

_____

_____

_____

Prayer:

_____

_____

_____

_____

_____

_____

_____

_____

_____

Memory Verse(s):

_____

_____

_____

_____

_____

_____

Day 9

Date: _____

Bible Passage: _____

Main ideas I see in this passage:

_____

_____

_____

_____

_____

_____

Key Verse(s):

_____

_____

_____

_____

_____

_____

Being a doer of the Word: What applications are there for me?

_____

_____

_____

_____

_____

_____

_____

_____

_____

_____

What sins should I confess and repent of through Christ?

_____

_____

_____

_____

_____

_____

What should I ask God to help me believe, think, and/or do?

_____

_____

_____

_____

_____

_____

_____

Prayer

Instruction:

_____

_____

_____

_____

_____

_____

_____

_____

Thanksgiving:

_____

_____

_____

_____

_____

_____

_____

_____

Confession:

_____

_____

_____

_____

_____

_____

_____

_____

_____

Prayer:

_____

_____

_____

_____

_____

_____

_____

Memory Verse(s):

_____

_____

_____

_____

_____

_____

Day 10

Date: _____

Bible Passage: _____

Main ideas I see in this passage:

_____

_____

_____

_____

_____

_____

Key Verse(s):

_____

_____

_____

_____

_____

_____

Being a doer of the Word: What applications are there for me?

_____

_____

_____

_____

_____

_____

_____

_____

_____

_____

What sins should I confess and repent of through Christ?

_____

_____

_____

_____

_____

_____

_____

What should I ask God to help me believe, think, and/or do?

_____

_____

_____

_____

_____

_____

_____

_____

Prayer

Instruction:

_____

_____

_____

_____

_____

_____

_____

_____

Thanksgiving:

_____

_____

_____

_____

_____

_____

_____

_____

Confession:

_____

_____

_____

_____

_____

_____

_____

_____

_____

Prayer:

_____

_____

_____

_____

_____

_____

_____

_____

Memory Verse(s):

_____

_____

_____

_____

_____

_____

Week Three

Sermon Notes

Date: _____

Preaching Passage: _____

Notes:

_____

_____

_____

_____

_____

_____

_____

_____

_____

_____

_____

_____

Applications:

_____

_____

_____

_____

_____

_____

Day 11

Date: _____

Bible Passage: _____

Main ideas I see in this passage:

_____
_____
_____
_____
_____
_____
_____

Key Verse(s):

_____
_____
_____
_____
_____
_____

Being a doer of the Word: What applications are there for me?

_____
_____
_____
_____

_____

_____

_____

_____

_____

_____

What sins should I confess and repent of through Christ?

_____

_____

_____

_____

_____

_____

_____

What should I ask God to help me believe, think, and/or do?

_____

_____

_____

_____

_____

_____

_____

_____

Prayer

Instruction:

_____
_____
_____
_____
_____
_____
_____
_____

Thanksgiving:

_____
_____
_____
_____
_____
_____
_____
_____

Confession:

_____
_____

_____

_____

_____

_____

_____

_____

_____

Prayer:

_____

_____

_____

_____

_____

_____

_____

_____

Memory Verse(s):

_____

_____

_____

_____

_____

_____

Day 12

Date: _____

Bible Passage: _____

Main ideas I see in this passage:

_____

_____

_____

_____

_____

_____

Key Verse(s):

_____

_____

_____

_____

_____

_____

Being a doer of the Word: What applications are there for me?

_____

_____

_____

_____

_____

_____

_____

_____

_____

_____

What sins should I confess and repent of through Christ?

_____

_____

_____

_____

_____

_____

_____

What should I ask God to help me believe, think, and/or do?

_____

_____

_____

_____

_____

_____

_____

_____

Prayer

Instruction:

_____

_____

_____

_____

_____

_____

_____

_____

_____

Thanksgiving:

_____

_____

_____

_____

_____

_____

_____

_____

_____

Confession:

_____

_____

_____

_____

_____

_____

_____

_____

_____

_____

Prayer:

_____

_____

_____

_____

_____

_____

_____

_____

_____

Memory Verse(s):

_____

_____

_____

_____

_____

_____

Day 13

Date: _____

Bible Passage: _____

Main ideas I see in this passage:

_____

_____

_____

_____

_____

_____

Key Verse(s):

_____

_____

_____

_____

_____

_____

Being a doer of the Word: What applications are there for me?

_____

_____

_____

_____

_____

_____

_____

_____

_____

_____

What sins should I confess and repent of through Christ?

_____

_____

_____

_____

_____

_____

_____

What should I ask God to help me believe, think, and/or do?

_____

_____

_____

_____

_____

_____

_____

_____

Prayer

Instruction:

_____

_____

_____

_____

_____

_____

_____

_____

Thanksgiving:

_____

_____

_____

_____

_____

_____

_____

_____

Confession:

_____

_____

_____

_____

_____

_____

_____

_____

_____

Prayer:

_____

_____

_____

_____

_____

_____

_____

_____

Memory Verse(s):

_____

_____

_____

_____

_____

_____

Day 14

Date: _____

Bible Passage: _____

Main ideas I see in this passage:

_____

_____

_____

_____

_____

_____

Key Verse(s):

_____

_____

_____

_____

_____

Being a doer of the Word: What applications are there for me?

_____

_____

_____

_____

_____

_____

_____

_____

_____

_____

What sins should I confess and repent of through Christ?

_____

_____

_____

_____

_____

_____

_____

What should I ask God to help me believe, think, and/or do?

_____

_____

_____

_____

_____

_____

_____

Prayer

Instruction:

_____

_____

_____

_____

_____

_____

_____

Thanksgiving:

_____

_____

_____

_____

_____

_____

_____

Confession:

_____

_____

_____

_____

_____

_____

_____

_____

_____

Prayer:

_____

_____

_____

_____

_____

_____

_____

Memory Verse(s):

_____

_____

_____

_____

_____

Day 15

Date: _____

Bible Passage: _____

Main ideas I see in this passage:

_____

_____

_____

_____

_____

_____

Key Verse(s):

_____

_____

_____

_____

_____

_____

Being a doer of the Word: What applications are there for me?

_____

_____

_____

_____

_____

_____

_____

_____

_____

_____

What sins should I confess and repent of through Christ?

_____

_____

_____

_____

_____

_____

_____

What should I ask God to help me believe, think, and/or do?

_____

_____

_____

_____

_____

_____

_____

_____

Prayer

Instruction:

_____

_____

_____

_____

_____

_____

_____

_____

_____

Thanksgiving:

_____

_____

_____

_____

_____

_____

_____

_____

_____

Confession:

_____

_____

_____

_____

_____

_____

_____

_____

_____

Prayer:

_____

_____

_____

_____

_____

_____

_____

Memory Verse(s):

_____

_____

_____

_____

_____

_____

Week Four

Sermon Notes

Date: _____

Preaching Passage: _____

Notes:

_____

_____

_____

_____

_____

_____

_____

_____

_____

_____

_____

Applications:

_____

_____

_____

_____

_____

Day 16

Date: _____

Bible Passage: _____

Main ideas I see in this passage:

_____

_____

_____

_____

_____

_____

Key Verse(s):

_____

_____

_____

_____

_____

Being a doer of the Word: What applications are there for me?

_____

_____

_____

_____

_____

_____

_____

_____

_____

_____

What sins should I confess and repent of through Christ?

_____

_____

_____

_____

_____

_____

_____

What should I ask God to help me believe, think, and/or do?

_____

_____

_____

_____

_____

_____

_____

_____

Prayer

Instruction:

_____

_____

_____

_____

_____

_____

_____

_____

Thanksgiving:

_____

_____

_____

_____

_____

_____

_____

_____

Confession:

_____

_____

_____

_____

_____

_____

_____

_____

_____

Prayer:

_____

_____

_____

_____

_____

_____

_____

_____

_____

Memory Verse(s):

_____

_____

_____

_____

_____

_____

Day 17

Date: _____

Bible Passage: _____

Main ideas I see in this passage:

_____

_____

_____

_____

_____

_____

Key Verse(s):

_____

_____

_____

_____

_____

_____

Being a doer of the Word: What applications are there for me?

_____

_____

_____

_____

_____

_____

_____

_____

_____

_____

What sins should I confess and repent of through Christ?

_____

_____

_____

_____

_____

_____

_____

What should I ask God to help me believe, think, and/or do?

_____

_____

_____

_____

_____

_____

_____

_____

Prayer

Instruction:

_____

_____

_____

_____

_____

_____

_____

_____

Thanksgiving:

_____

_____

_____

_____

_____

_____

_____

_____

Confession:

_____

_____

_____
_____
_____
_____
_____
_____
_____

Prayer:

_____
_____
_____
_____
_____
_____
_____
_____

Memory Verse(s):

_____
_____
_____
_____
_____
_____

Day 18

Date: _____

Bible Passage: _____

Main ideas I see in this passage:

_____

_____

_____

_____

_____

Key Verse(s):

_____

_____

_____

_____

_____

Being a doer of the Word: What applications are there for me?

_____

_____

_____

_____

_____

_____

_____

_____

_____

_____

What sins should I confess and repent of through Christ?

_____

_____

_____

_____

_____

_____

_____

What should I ask God to help me believe, think, and/or do?

_____

_____

_____

_____

_____

_____

_____

_____

Prayer

Instruction:

_____

_____

_____

_____

_____

_____

_____

_____

Thanksgiving:

_____

_____

_____

_____

_____

_____

_____

_____

Confession:

_____

_____

_____

_____

_____

_____

_____

_____

_____

Prayer:

_____

_____

_____

_____

_____

_____

_____

_____

Memory Verse(s):

_____

_____

_____

_____

_____

_____

Day 19

Date: _____

Bible Passage: _____

Main ideas I see in this passage:

_____

_____

_____

_____

_____

_____

Key Verse(s):

_____

_____

_____

_____

_____

_____

Being a doer of the Word: What applications are there for me?

_____

_____

_____

_____

_____

_____

_____

_____

_____

_____

What sins should I confess and repent of through Christ?

_____

_____

_____

_____

_____

_____

_____

_____

What should I ask God to help me believe, think, and/or do?

_____

_____

_____

_____

_____

_____

_____

_____

_____

Prayer

Instruction:

_____

_____

_____

_____

_____

_____

_____

_____

_____

Thanksgiving:

_____

_____

_____

_____

_____

_____

_____

_____

_____

Confession:

_____

_____

_____

_____

_____

_____

_____

_____

_____

Prayer:

_____

_____

_____

_____

_____

_____

_____

_____

_____

Memory Verse(s):

_____

_____

_____

_____

_____

_____

Day 20

Date: _____

Bible Passage: _____

Main ideas I see in this passage:

_____

_____

_____

_____

_____

_____

Key Verse(s):

_____

_____

_____

_____

_____

Being a doer of the Word: What applications are there for me?

_____

_____

_____

_____

_____

_____

_____

_____

_____

_____

_____

What sins should I confess and repent of through Christ?

_____

_____

_____

_____

_____

_____

_____

_____

What should I ask God to help me believe, think, and/or do?

_____

_____

_____

_____

_____

_____

_____

_____

Prayer

Instruction:

_____
_____
_____
_____
_____
_____
_____
_____

Thanksgiving:

_____
_____
_____
_____
_____
_____
_____
_____

Confession:

_____
_____

_____

_____

_____

_____

_____

_____

_____

Prayer:

_____

_____

_____

_____

_____

_____

_____

_____

Memory Verse(s):

_____

_____

_____

_____

_____

_____

Where to Go from Here

If you've meditated on Scripture and prayed through this journal to the end, congratulations! I truly hope that this has been an enriching way for you to grow to enjoy God more and have a "game plan" for coming to His Word prayerfully each day.

It is impossible to overestimate the role of the Bible in knowing God and becoming more like Christ. In one of my favorite passages about how believers are being transformed into the image of Christ, Paul writes, "Now the Lord is the Spirit; and where the Spirit of the Lord is, there is liberty. But we all, with unveiled face, beholding as in a mirror the glory of the Lord, are being transformed into the same image from glory to glory, just as by the Spirit of the Lord" (2 Corinthians 3:17-18). Whether you are in biblical counseling or not, meeting God in His Word is one of the primary means by which God is forming and shaping you. Jesus prayed to the Father, "Sanctify them by Your truth. Your word is truth" (John 17:17).

This journal is meant as a start to a "new normal." You may not continue to meditate and pray precisely the way this journal has laid out, but I hope that you have developed a habit of spending time with the Lord daily. So where do you go from here? *Keep going!* If you have been assigned this journal as part of your counseling, your counselor will help you in the next steps. But whatever the case, may it be with us as Hosea proclaimed:

"Let us know; let us press on to know the LORD"
(Hosea 6:3a, ESV)

Made in the USA
Las Vegas, NV
01 December 2023